SPORTS
COLORING BOOK FOR KIDS

This coloring book belongs to:

_____

SOPHIA SIEGERT

Hey there, amazing parents!

We're thrilled that you've chosen our Sports Coloring Book for your kids. To show our appreciation, we've added a special gift just for you!

Simply grab your smartphone, open the camera, point it at the **QR code**, and watch the magic happen! You'll instantly unlock **a FREE Sports Quiz** based on our Coloring Book. It's a fun and educational way to engage with your kids and see just how much they've absorbed from our Sports Coloring Book. Happy quizzing!

SCAN ME

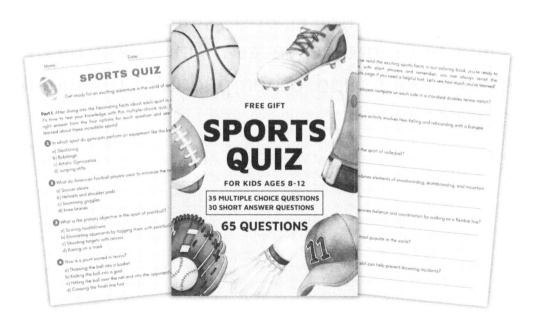

Get Your Free Gift

AMERICAN FOOTBALL

American Football evolved from various forms of rugby and soccer in the late 19th century. It has since become one of the most popular sports in the United States, with a rich history and a passionate fan base.

It is a highly physical and contact-driven sport. Players wear protective gear, including helmets, shoulder pads, and other padding, to minimize the risk of injury.

ARCHERY

Archery is one of the oldest arts still practiced today, with evidence of its use dating back thousands of years. It played a significant role in hunting and warfare throughout history.

The legendary character Robin Hood is often associated with archery. While the stories about Robin Hood vary, he is commonly depicted as a skilled archer who robbed the rich to help the poor.

ARTISTIC GYMNASTICS

Introduced in 1894, artistic gymnastics was one of the original disciplines in the modern Olympic Games. Artistic gymnasts are challenged to perfect their skills across a range of equipment, such as the beam and performing on the floor.

Artistic gymnastics has seen legendary athletes who have made significant contributions to the sport. Icons such as Nadia Comăneci, Olga Korbut, Simone Biles, and Kohei Uchimura are celebrated for their record-breaking performances.

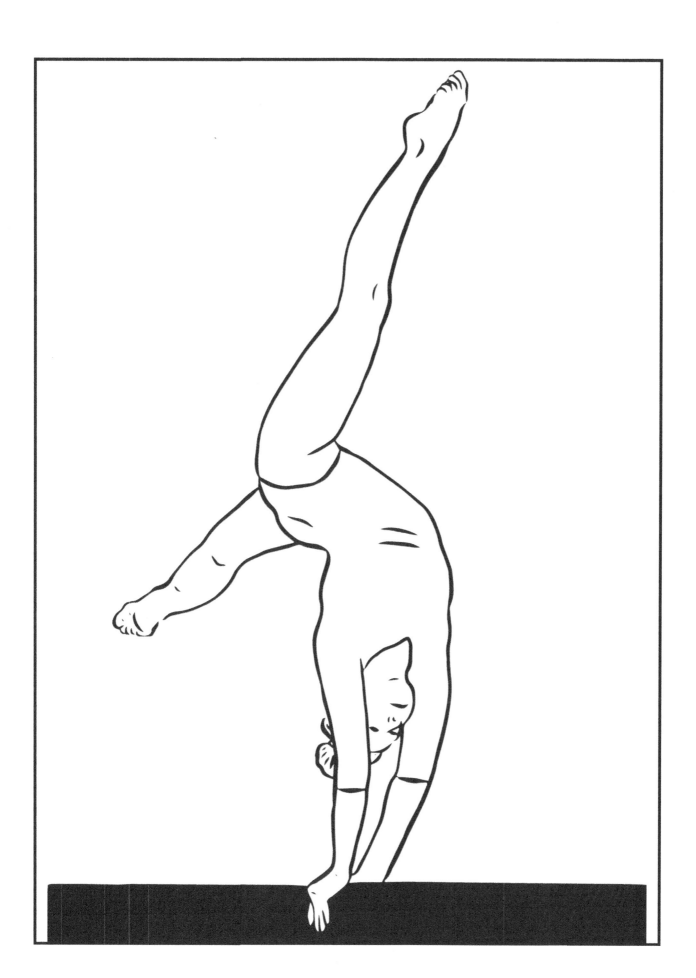

BASEBALL

Baseball traces its roots back to early bat-and-ball games played in England and North America. The modern version of baseball developed in the mid-19th century and has since become one of the most popular sports in the United States.

Baseball holds a prominent place in American culture and is often referred to as the "national pastime." It has inspired literature, films, music, and artwork, becoming a symbol of nostalgia and community.

BASKETBALL

Basketball was invented in December 1891 by Dr. James Naismith, a Canadian physical education instructor, while he was teaching at the YMCA in Springfield, Massachusetts. It was originally created as a way to keep his students active indoors during the winter.

Basketball has been an Olympic sport since 1936. The United States has been particularly dominant in Olympic basketball, winning numerous gold medals, and producing legendary players like Michael Jordan, Magic Johnson, and Kobe Bryant.

BOBSLEIGH

Bobsleigh originated in the late 19th century in Switzerland as a way for people to travel quickly down snowy slopes. It evolved into a competitive sport and made its Olympic debut in 1924.

Bobsleigh is known for its high speeds. Athletes can reach speeds exceeding 120 kilometers per hour (75 mph) on certain tracks, making it one of the fastest sports in the Winter Olympics.

BOXING

Boxing has ancient roots, dating back over 5,000 years to ancient civilizations like Egypt and Mesopotamia. It was also a popular sport in ancient Greece, where it was included in the Olympic Games. Boxing has been a part of the modern Olympic Games since 1904.

Boxing has seen many legendary fighters throughout history. Some of the most famous boxers include Muhammad Ali, Mike Tyson, Sugar Ray Robinson, Joe Louis, Floyd Mayweather Jr., Manny Pacquiao, and many others.

BUNGEE JUMPING

Bungee jumping is known for providing an exhilarating adrenaline rush. The feeling of free-falling and the rebounding sensation when the bungee cord reaches its maximum stretch can be both thrilling and exciting for participants.

Safety is a top priority in bungee jumping. Operators ensure the use of high-quality equipment, including strong cords, harnesses, and safety backup systems. Regular inspections and maintenance are conducted to ensure participant safety.

CRICKET

Cricket has ancient origins, with its roots traced back to 16th-century England. The sport evolved from various ball-and-bat games played during that time. It is one of the most popular sports globally, particularly in countries like India, England, Australia, Pakistan, South Africa, and the West Indies.

Cricket is often referred to as the "Gentleman's Game" due to its emphasis on sportsmanship and fair play. The players are expected to adhere to a code of conduct, respect the umpires' decisions, and uphold the spirit of fair competition.

CURLING

Curling traces its origins back to medieval Scotland, where it was played on frozen ponds and lochs as early as the 16th century. The sport has since evolved and gained international popularity.

Curling is sometimes referred to as "The Roaring Game" due to the sound made by the sliding stones as they move across the ice. The friction between the stone and the ice creates a distinctive rumbling noise.

CYCLING

The Tour de France is one of the most prestigious bicycle races in the world. It was first held in 1903 and takes place annually, covering approximately 3,500 kilometers (2,200 miles) over a three-week period.

There are various types of bicycles designed for different purposes. These include road bikes, mountain bikes, hybrid bikes, cyclocross bikes, BMX bikes, and more, each with specific features suited for their intended use.

Field Hockey

The modern version of field hockey originated in England in the 19th century. Field hockey is an Olympic sport and has been a part of the Olympic Games since 1908 for men and 1980 for women.

Field hockey is known for its fast-paced gameplay, requiring quick thinking, agility, and endurance from the players. The ball can travel at high speeds, and the game often involves rapid passing, dribbling, and changes in direction.

ICE CLIMBING

Ice climbing is an adventurous activity that involves ascending frozen ice formations such as waterfalls, glaciers, and ice walls. It requires climbers to use specialized equipment and techniques to ascend icy surfaces.

Safety is a paramount concern in ice climbing. Climbers use various safety measures, including the use of ropes, harnesses, and protective helmets. Belaying techniques and anchor systems are employed to ensure the safety of climbers and their partners.

ICE HOCKEY

Ice hockey is known for its fast-paced nature. The game moves quickly, with players skating at high speeds, making swift passes, and shooting the puck with force. Ice hockey is played at various international competitions, including the Winter Olympics.

It is a physically demanding sport that involves body-checking, stick-checking, and other forms of physical contact. Players wear protective gear, including helmets, pads, and mouthguards, to minimize the risk of injury.

JUMPING STILTS (POWERBOCKING)

Jumping stilts, also known as Powerbocks or Powerbocking, were invented by a German aerospace engineer named Alexander Böck in the late 1990s. Böck designed and developed the stilts to provide a unique jumping experience.

Jumping stilts are unique in that they incorporate spring-loaded mechanisms that store and release energy with each step. The springs, typically made of fiberglass or carbon fiber, provide a rebound effect, allowing users to jump and bounce to impressive heights.

KARATE

The term "karate" translates to "empty hand" in Japanese. It signifies the martial art's emphasis on unarmed combat techniques, using only the practitioner's body for defense and offense.

Karate utilizes a belt ranking system to indicate a practitioner's level of skill and experience. The most commonly recognized belt colors, in order of progression from beginner to advanced, are white, yellow, orange, green, blue, brown, and black.

MONSTER TRUCK

Monster truck competitions began in the late 1970s in the United States. The sport emerged from events called "car crushing" and evolved into organized shows featuring modified trucks with giant wheels and powerful engines.

Safety is a top priority in monster truck events. Trucks are equipped with roll cages and other safety features to protect drivers during accidents or rollovers. Tracks are built with safety measures in place, and strict rules and regulations govern the sport.

MOTOCROSS

Motocross originated in the United Kingdom in the early 20th century as a form of motorcycle racing. It was initially conducted on off-road tracks and later evolved into a distinct discipline. It involves racing on a closed circuit track that features various obstacles, including jumps, berms, whoops, and uneven terrain.

Motocross requires a combination of skill, technique, physical fitness, and mental focus. Riders must navigate the challenging track, maintain control over the bike, and perform jumps and turns with precision and speed. Riders wear specialized gear to ensure safety and protection.

MOUNTAIN BIKING

Mountain biking originated in the 1970s in Marin County, California, USA. It evolved as a result of riders modifying cruiser bikes to tackle off-road trails and has since become a popular outdoor activity.

Mountain biking has become a popular tourism activity, with destinations around the world offering world-class trails and riding experiences. Locations such as Whistler in Canada, Moab in the United States, and Rotorua in New Zealand have gained recognition among mountain bike enthusiasts.

MOUNTAIN BOARDING

Mountain boarding, also known as all-terrain boarding, was developed in the 1990s as an off-road alternative to snowboarding. It combines elements of snowboarding, skateboarding, and mountain biking.

Given the potential for high speeds and challenging terrain, protective gear is essential in mountain boarding. Riders typically wear helmets, knee pads, elbow pads, wrist guards, and other protective equipment to minimize the risk of injuries.

PAINTBALL

Paintball originated in the 1980s as a recreational activity but quickly evolved into a competitive sport. It was initially used by forestry groups and ranchers to mark trees and livestock, eventually transitioning into a game of strategy and skill.

Paintball is a team-based sport where players compete to eliminate opponents by tagging them with paint-filled gelatin capsules, commonly known as paintballs. The objective is to eliminate all members of the opposing team or complete specific mission objectives.

PARAGLIDING

Paragliding is a recreational and competitive flying sport that allows participants to fly through the air without the use of an engine. Instead, paragliders harness the power of wind and thermal updrafts to stay aloft.

Paragliding prioritizes safety, and pilots use safety equipment, such as reserve parachutes, helmets, and safety harnesses. Regular training, understanding weather conditions, and adhering to safety guidelines are essential to minimize risks.

RALLY RACING

Rally racing is an off-road motorsport that involves racing on various terrains, including gravel, dirt, mud, snow, and tarmac. It is known for its challenging courses and unpredictable conditions.

Rally races consist of multiple timed stages, where drivers compete against the clock to complete a specific section of the course. The combined times from all stages determine the overall winner of the race.

ROLLER SKATING

Roller skating provides a fun and engaging way to improve cardiovascular fitness, balance, coordination, and muscular strength. It is a low-impact activity that can be enjoyed by people of various ages and fitness levels.

Roller skating has been part of the Olympic program in the past. It was included as a demonstration sport in the 1992 Barcelona Olympics and as a full medal sport in the 1908 London Olympics.

ROWING

Rowing is one of the oldest known sports, with evidence of rowing competitions dating back to ancient Egypt and Greece. It was also a popular mode of transportation in many civilizations.

Rowing requires strong teamwork and coordination among rowers. The sport fosters a sense of camaraderie and trust as rowers work together to achieve a shared goal of propelling the boat efficiently and winning races.

RUGBY

Rugby originated in England in the early 19th century. It is believed to have evolved from various forms of football played at the time, with the Rugby School in Rugby, Warwickshire playing a significant role in its development.

Rugby is known for its physicality and full-contact nature. It requires strength, speed, agility, and endurance. Tackling, rucking, scrummaging, and mauling are integral parts of the game.

SKATEBOARDING

Skateboarding originated in California, United States, in the late 1940s and early 1950s. It was initially influenced by surfing and was primarily practiced by surfers on days when the waves were not suitable for riding.

Skateboarding is renowned for its wide range of tricks and maneuvers. From basic tricks like ollies, kickflips, and grinds to more advanced aerial tricks and complex combinations, skateboarders continuously push the boundaries of what is possible on a skateboard.

SKIING

Skiing is one of the oldest known sports, with evidence of skiing dating back over 4,000 years. The earliest skis were used for practical purposes like transportation and hunting in snowy regions.

Skiing requires specialized equipment, including skis, boots, bindings, and poles. Skis are designed for specific types of skiing and come in various lengths, widths, and shapes to suit different terrains and skill levels.

SKYDIVING

The typical altitude for skydiving is between 10,000 and 15,000 feet (3,000 to 4,500 meters) above ground level. At this altitude, skydivers have enough time for freefall and to deploy their parachutes safely.

Safety is of utmost importance in skydiving. Skydiving centers have strict regulations, training programs, and equipment checks in place to ensure the safety of participants. Skydivers use specially designed parachutes and wear safety gear like helmets and altimeters.

SLACKLINING

Slacklining emerged in the late 1970s as a practice among rock climbers in Yosemite National Park, California, USA. They would set up climbing webbing (slackline) between two anchor points to balance and walk on.

Slacklining is an excellent activity for improving balance, coordination, and core strength. Maintaining stability and control on the flexible line engages various muscle groups and promotes overall body awareness.

SNOWBOARDING

Snowboarding emerged as a sport in the 1960s and 1970s. It was heavily influenced by skateboarding, surfing, and skiing. The first commercial snowboard was invented in 1965 by Sherman Poppen and was called the "Snurfer."

Snowboarding encompasses various styles of riding, including freestyle, freeride, and alpine. Freestyle snowboarding focuses on tricks, jumps, and terrain park features, while freeride emphasizes exploring the mountain and riding natural terrain. Alpine snowboarding involves carving precise turns and high-speed descents.

SOCCER (FOOTBALL)

Soccer, also known as football, is the most popular sport in the world, with a fanbase that spans across continents. It is estimated that more than 4 billion people worldwide consider themselves soccer fans.

Soccer has produced numerous iconic players who have achieved legendary status in the sport. Players like Pelé, Diego Maradona, Johan Cruyff, Cristiano Ronaldo, and Lionel Messi have left a lasting impact on the game and garnered international fame.

SPRINTING

In sprinting races, the start is crucial. Sprinters aim to react quickly to the starting gun, but false starts can result in disqualification. Athletes strive for a balance between a quick reaction time and avoiding false starts.

Sprinters focus on maximizing their speed by utilizing proper technique. This includes an explosive start, driving knee lift, powerful arm swing, and efficient stride length. Sprinters also work on their acceleration, maintaining top speed, and finishing strong.

SURFING

Surfing has a vibrant and unique culture associated with it. It embodies a laid-back lifestyle, a connection with nature, and an appreciation for ocean conservation. Surfing culture encompasses art, music, fashion, and a sense of camaraderie among surfers.

Surfers follow an unwritten code of etiquette known as the "Surfer's Code." It includes respecting other surfers in the water, taking turns, avoiding drop-ins (stealing someone's wave), and prioritizing safety and good sportsmanship.

SWIMMING

Swimming has been a part of the modern Olympic Games since the inaugural edition in 1896. It is one of the most popular and widely watched sports in the Olympic program.

Learning to swim is not only a recreational activity but also an essential life skill. The ability to swim can help prevent drowning incidents and provides individuals with the confidence to enjoy water activities safely.

TENNIS

Tennis has roots that can be traced back to 12th-century France, where it was played by hitting a ball with the palm of the hand. The sport evolved over the centuries, and the modern game we know today emerged in the 19th century.

Tennis can be played in singles, where one player competes against another, or in doubles, where teams of two players compete against each other. Doubles matches require different strategies and teamwork.

VOLLEYBALL

Volleyball was invented in 1895 by William G. Morgan, a physical education instructor, in Massachusetts, United States. Initially called "mintonette," the sport was created as an indoor game combining elements of basketball, tennis, and handball.

Beach volleyball is a popular variant of the sport played on sand courts. It gained worldwide recognition and became an Olympic event in 1996. Beach volleyball is known for its fast-paced and dynamic nature, with two-player teams competing in exciting matches.

WALL CLIMBING

Wall climbing, also known as rock climbing or indoor climbing, has its roots in mountaineering and outdoor rock climbing. It emerged as a distinct sport in the mid-20th century and gained popularity as a recreational and competitive activity.

Wall climbing is a physically demanding sport that requires strength, flexibility, balance, and endurance. It also challenges climbers mentally, as they navigate routes, problem-solve, and overcome fears and obstacles.

WATER POLO

Water polo is a dynamic and physically demanding sport. Players must constantly swim, tread water, pass, shoot, and defend against opponents. The game requires strength, endurance, agility, and strong swimming skills.

Players in water polo wear caps to distinguish between teams and positions. One team wears white caps, while the other wears blue or dark caps. The goalkeeper wears a red cap to identify their role.

WEIGHTLIFTING

Weightlifting is a sport that requires both raw strength and explosive power. Athletes undergo rigorous strength training programs to develop their muscles and increase their capacity to lift heavy weights.

Weightlifting is not solely about strength; it also involves mastering proper technique and skill. Lifters must focus on balance, timing, and precise movements to execute the lifts correctly and maximize their lifting potential.

WHITE WATER KAYAKING

White water kayaking is a thrilling and adventurous water sport that involves navigating rivers and rapids in a kayak. It requires skill, technique, and physical agility to navigate through the fast-moving and turbulent waters.

White water kayaking offers the opportunity to explore and experience beautiful and remote river locations. It allows kayakers to connect with nature, navigate stunning landscapes, and encounter wildlife along their paddling journeys.

WHITE WATER RAFTING

White water rafting is an exhilarating adventure sport that involves navigating rivers and rapids in an inflatable raft. It is a thrilling activity that combines teamwork, skill, and a love for adventure.

Safety is a top priority in white water rafting. Rafters are equipped with personal flotation devices (PFDs), helmets, and appropriate protective gear. Guides also play a crucial role in ensuring safety by providing instructions, rescue techniques, and knowledge of the river.

YOGA

Yoga incorporates mindfulness and meditation techniques to cultivate present-moment awareness and inner calm. These practices help individuals develop a deeper connection between the body, mind, and breath.

Yoga offers numerous benefits for both the body and mind. Regular practice can improve flexibility, strength, balance, and posture. It also promotes relaxation, reduces stress, enhances mental clarity, and cultivates mindfulness.

COLOR TEST PAGE

13877138R00052